Experiments with

FORCES

TREVOR COOK

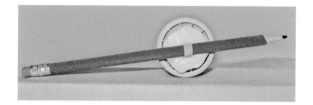

PowerKiDS
press.

New York

Published in 2009 by The Rosen Publishing Group, Inc.
29 East 21st Street, New York, NY 10010

Editor: Alex Woolf
Designers: Sally Henry and Trevor Cook
Consultant: Keith Clayson
U.S. Editor: Kara Murray

Picture Credits: Sally Henry and Trevor Cook

Every attempt has been made to clear copyright. Should there be any
inadvertent omission, please apply to the publisher for rectification.

Library of Congress Cataloging-in-Publication Data

Cook, Trevor.
  Experiments with forces / Trevor Cook.
     p. cm. — (Science lab)
  Includes index.
  ISBN 978-1-4358-2804-9 (library binding) — ISBN 978-1-4358-3217-6 (pbk.)
ISBN 978-1-4042-8022-9 (6-pack)
  1. Force and energy—Experiments—Juvenile literature. I. Title.
  QC73.4.C657 2009
  531'.6—dc22
                              2008036888

Printed in the United States

Contents

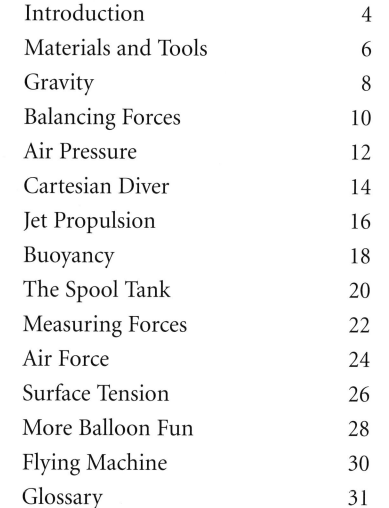

Introduction

Forces are involved in everything we do. When we make something move, we are in control of some forces and have to respond to others, often without knowing what they are! It can be gravity, magnetism, or anything that causes a push or a pull.

Sir Isaac Newton's laws of motion were published in 1687 and deal with *inertia*, the relationship between mass and *velocity* (*momentum*) and the forces acting on objects. We'll look at gravity on page 8.

Since ancient times, scientists have used the idea of forces to try to explain the workings of everything from simple machinery to the movements of the planets. Over 4,000 years ago, the builders of Stonehenge seem to have placed the stones according to very careful *observations* of the stars and their movements.

At the CERN laboratory in Switzerland, scientists study the *interaction* of the tiniest of particles.

Archimedes, a Greek scientist and mathematician from Syracuse, in what is now Italy, was asked by King Hero II to find out whether a new crown was made of solid gold, or if it had silver in it. Knowing the *density* of gold, he needed to find the *volume* of the crown. He found out the answer when he stepped into his bath and displaced his own volume of water. If he *submerged* the crown and measured the displaced water, he could figure out the the crown's volume.

In the ocean between Japan and Papua New Guinea, the Mariana Trench is the deepest water yet measured, at over 36,000 feet (11,000 m). The pressure at this depth is well over 1,000 times that at the surface. We'll use pressure to send our diver to the bottom on pages 14–15.

Orville and Wilbur Wright's first controlled, powered and *sustained* heavier-than-air human flight in 1903 traveled just 119.8 feet (36.5 m). Balancing the forces of power, drag, *lift* and gravity remains the main thing that aircraft designers have to do. Test our design on page 24 and see if you can improve on it!

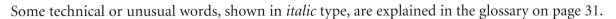

Some technical or unusual words, shown in *italic* type, are explained in the glossary on page 31.

Materials and Tools

For our experiments, you may have to buy a few things from a store but you should easily find most of what you need around the house.

20 minutes

This tells you about how long a project should take.

This symbol means you might need adult help.

Plasticine If you don't already have some of this popular modeling material, you can get it from a good crafts shop.

Scissors Ask an adult for an old pair of scissors that you can keep for all your experiments.

They will be very useful. Keep them away from young children.

Plastic bottles Ask an adult for empty plastic bottles. The ones used for water and soda are best.

Paints and brushes Poster paints or ready-mixed colors can be bought at crafts shops.

String Household string will be fine for our use, but you can also use nylon fishing line, often stocked by sports shops (see page 16).

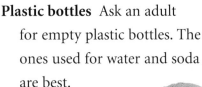

Tape We use tape to hold things in position. A tape dispenser makes it easier to work with,

Funnel is very useful for filtering liquids or when filling bottles.

Packing tape When we need to make stronger connections, it's best to use wider, brown tape, which is good securing cardboard.

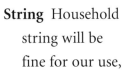

Glue stick is mostly used for sticking paper to paper. Rubber cement is a rubbery glue that sticks most things to most other things!

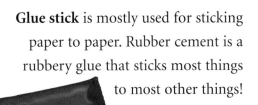

Straws We'll need some plastic drinking straws. Try the kitchen drawer!

Colored markers

You will find it handy to have a box of colored markers for several of the projects.

Balloons Keep some balloons after your next party, but you may need to buy an especially large one to do the experiment on page 28.

Thread You will need some strong sewing thread. Ask permission to use some.

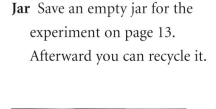

Scales Ask an adult if you can borrow some kitchen scales.

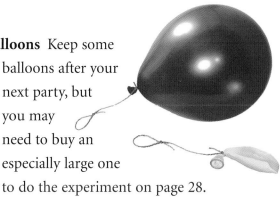

Jar Save an empty jar for the experiment on page 13. Afterward you can recycle it.

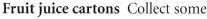

Stiff wire Often sold in small coils, is needed for the balancing acts on pages 10–11.

Notebook Keep a special notebook to record the results of your experiments.

Fruit juice cartons Collect some 1-liter cartons from your kitchen. Wash them out with water before use.

Glass marbles You will need some weights for testing on pages 22–23. Marbles will be ideal.

Wax candle Find an ordinary candle to make a washer for your tank on page 20.

Eyedropper This is cheap to buy from a pharmacy.

Friends can help

Do the experiments with your friends when you can, especially when you need assistants!

Corks Ask an adult to save you a few corks from wine bottles.

Gravity

All objects are drawn to each other and the larger the object the larger the force. The Earth is huge and so has a very large force, which we call gravity.

You will need:

- foam cup, water
- stepladder or something you can stand on safely, old ballpoint pen
- small plastic bucket
- somewhere outside to do the experiments

The plan

We are going to see how gravity pulls objects toward the Earth, then look at a way to beat it!

Experiment 1

1 Make a small hole with a pen in the side of the cup near the base.

2 Fill the cup with water. See how the water runs out.

3 Cover the hole with your finger and fill the cup again. Stand on the stepladder and drop the cup of water.

What's going on?

Gravity makes the cup and the water *accelerate* down at the same rate. They fall together and the water stays in the cup till they hit the ground.

Experiment 2

1 Half fill your bucket with water.　**2** Outside, swing the bucket forward and back. Increase the swing and make sure you don't spill any water.

What's going on?

When you swing the bucket, you apply a centrifugal force to the water in addition to gravity. The faster you swing, the greater the centrifugal force. When it's great enough, the water will stay in the bucket, regardless of gravity.

Jargon Buster

"**Centrifugal**" means "moving away from the center."

3 When you get near the top of the swing, try going right over the top in a complete circle!

Balancing Forces

When gravity pulls on an object, it appears to be acting on a single point, which is called the center of gravity.

You will need:

- 2 corks, stiff wire
- plasticine, cardboard
- rubber cement
- toothpicks
- scissors
- marker
- fishing line
- plastic straw
- chair, table

The plan

We are going to make objects with the center of gravity in unexpected places.

Experiment 1

1 Draw an outline of a head and body to fit the width of your cork.

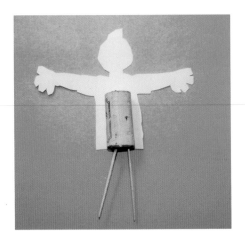

push through

bend and push back

2 Cut out the figure and glue it to the cork. Push the toothpicks into the cork for legs.

3 Ask an adult to cut a piece of wire 8 inches (200 mm) long. Bend it into a curve, add the plasticine and fix it to the cork.

4 Adjust the amount of plasticine to get your figure to balance.

What's going on?

The plasticine makes the center of gravity lower than the surface of the table.

Experiment 2

Cut little slits here . . .

. . . and here, so the arms can hold the pole.

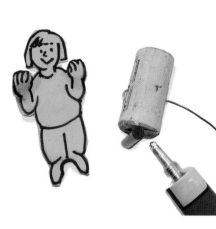

1 Make up a new cork with wire and a plasticine weight as in experiment 1.

2 Draw and cut out another little figure to fit on the cork. See how the feet are drawn.

3 Stick a piece of straw, about .8 inch (20 mm) long, to the base of the cork. Stick your figure on it.

4 Thread the fishing line through the straw, then tie it between two fixed points to make a sloping tightrope. We used our cupboard door handles. Finish your tightrope walker with a balancing pole made from a straw.

What's going on?

This time gravity can pull the figure down, so it slides down the line. The figure remains upright because its center of gravity is below the line.

Jargon Buster

A **sense of balance** prevents humans and animals from falling over!

Air Pressure

Although air is very light, there is a layer more than 60 miles (100 km) thick above us. This means there is a force of 15 pounds on every square inch (about 1 kg per square cm) on the surface of the Earth.

30 minutes

You will need:

- ruler
- sheet of paper
- table
- jar
- balloon

The plan
We are going to show the pressure of this layer of air on us.

Experiment 1

1 Use a sturdy table. Put the ruler on the table with a quarter of it hanging over the edge. Tap the end of the ruler with your finger so that it flips up. Make sure not to break anything!

2 Put the ruler back in the same place on the table. Lay a sheet of paper over the ruler to cover at least half of it. Tap the end of the ruler again. Try to use the same amount of force as you did in step 1.

What's going on?

The downward force of air on the paper resists the ruler flipping up!

Experiment 2

1 Challenge a friend to lift the jar with the balloon. When they say it's impossible, show them how with air pressure!

2 Put most of the balloon into the jar and start to blow it up.

3 As the balloon *inflates*, it gets forced into the shape of the jar.

4 Soon you can lift the jar by lifting the balloon!

What's going on?

Air pressure forces the balloon against the inside of the jar. As long as you hold the neck of the balloon tightly and keep the air in, you can easily lift the jar.

Jargon Buster

In physics, pressure is the force acting on an area, perpendicular to the surface. It is measured in **newtons** per square metre, known as **pascals.**

Cartesian Diver

Pressure is a force that pushes against something. Pressure on a material forces its *molecules* closer together and it becomes denser. As material becomes denser, it becomes heavier.

You will need:

- plastic bottle with lid
- plasticine
- eyedropper
- water container for testing
- water

The plan

We are going to show what happens when gases and liquids are put under pressure. It's a famous experiment, and we think it's fun!

What to do:

open end

Air is trapped in here.

1 Seal the air inside the dropper with a blob of plasticine, which will also act as a weight.

2 Test the buoyancy of your diver in water. It should only just float. Add or remove plasticine till you get it exactly right.

Jargon Buster

"**Cartesian**" relates to the French scientist and thinker René Descartes. The experiment is named in his honor.

3 We've used the same amount of plasticine in two colors and made a head and legs.

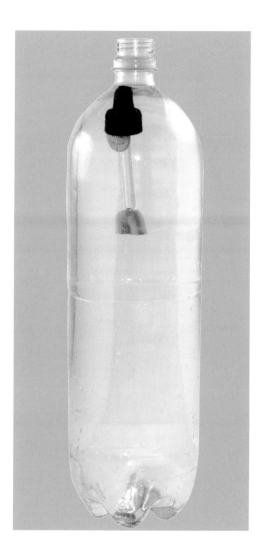

4 Fill the bottle with water. Put the diver in the bottle. Check that the diver is floating properly.

5 Screw the lid on tightly and squeeze the bottle. Your diver should move down in the bottle.

What's going on?

When the bottle is squeezed, everything inside is put under increased pressure. Water is denser than air and is harder to compress, so the air compresses much more than the water. At the start, the diver displaced only its own weight of water. When the air is compressed, it takes up less space and the diver displaces less than its own weight of water. When the pressure is released, he floats back up!

What else can you do?

Try making divers out of other things, such as pen tops, toys or balloons. Remember, you must have some air in your diver that can't escape.

Jargon Buster
"**Compress**" means "to squeeze something into less space."

15

Jet Propulsion

30 minutes

We think of the jet engine as being a modern invention, but the first one was invented by Hero of Alexandria in the first century AD.

Hero's engine

You will need:

- balloon (sausage shaped)
- plastic straw
- fishing line or fine string
- binder clip, tape
- empty fruit juice carton
- water, funnel
- old ballpoint pen
- somewhere outdoors

Experiment 1

The plan

We're going to show how a jet engine works.

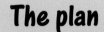

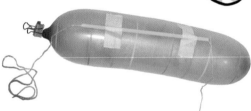

1 Thread the fishing line or string through the straw.

2 Inflate the balloon, then put the binder clip on the neck to keep the air in.

3 Tape the straw to the balloon. Tie each end of the line to something fixed, at least 20 feet (6 m) apart.

4 Release the clip!

What's going on?

The air inside the balloon is under pressure caused by the balloon trying to go back to its original shape. When the clip is released, air escapes through the neck, and the balloon is pushed in the opposite direction.

What else can you do?

Try using a balloon to make your toy cars or boats move!

Experiment 2

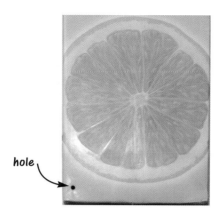

hole

1 Open the top flaps of the fruit juice carton and make small holes in them. Attach a loop of string between the flaps and another to the exact middle of the first string.

2 Make a hole in the front of the carton in the bottom left corner with the ballpoint pen. Make a similar hole on the other side.

3 From here on, it's best to work outside! Cover the holes with your finger and thumb and fill the carton with water. You might need an assistant for this.

4 Hold the carton up by the string and uncover the holes.

What's going on?

The force of the escaping water on opposite sides drives the carton around in a circle, with the string acting as a pivot. We're using gravity and water to make jet *propulsion*!

direction of rotation

water

Buoyancy

35 minutes

If we drop a piece of metal into water, it sinks. So how is it that a ship made of material that's heavier than water can float?

You will need:

- plasticine, paper clips
- water
- egg
- glass, pitcher
- salt
- tablespoon

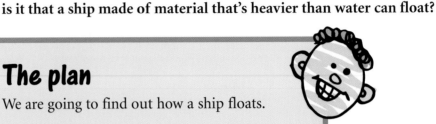

The plan

We are going to find out how a ship floats.

Experiment 1

1 Knead a piece of plasticine into the size and shape of a golf ball.

2 Fill the pitcher with water, then drop the plasticine ball into it. It sinks!

3 Take the ball out of the water, and dry it. Then form it into a hollow shape.

4 Carefully lower the plasticine shape into the water again.

5 Your boat will even carry cargo!

What's going on?

Plasticine is much denser than water so, in step 1, it sinks. If you've managed to enclose enough space in your shape, it will float on the water. Archimedes discovered that an object will float when it displaces more than its own weight of water (see page 5).

Jargon Buster
"**Displace**" means "to take the place of."

Experiment 2

1 Half fill the pitcher with water and add about six tablespoons of salt. Stir it well to dissolve the salt.

2 Fill it up with plain water. Pour the water over a spoon so as not to mix it with the salt water.

3 Carefully lower the egg into the glass using the spoon. Try not to make a splash!

4 The egg floats halfway down into the pitcher!

What's going on?

The egg is denser than plain water but less dense than salt water. So it floats at the boundary between the two. It has buoyancy in the salt water but not in the plain water.

Jargon Buster

Buoyancy describes the ability to rise in a gas or liquid.

The Spool Tank

We often need to store energy so that it is available exactly when we need it. Gasoline and batteries are examples of stored energy. Our bodies take in other forms of stored energy when we eat.

You will need:

- long pencil
- rubber band
- empty thread spool
- piece of candle
- paper clip, craft knife

The plan

We are going to make a toy that uses stored energy to make it move. We call it a tank.

Experiment 1

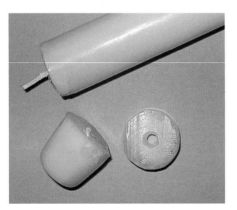
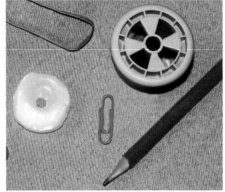

1 Get an adult to cut a piece off the candle. Make a hole in it.

2 Assemble the pieces. Push the rubber band through the thread spool and attach the paper clip.

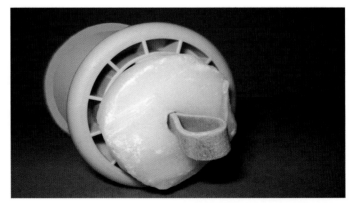

3 Thread the rubber band through the candle.

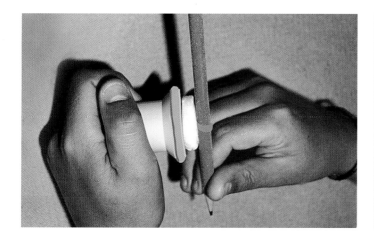

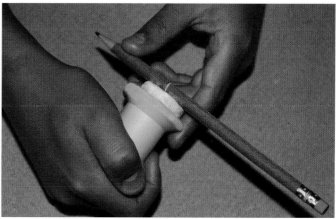

4 Put the pencil through the rubber band and wind it up as tightly as you can without breaking the band.

5 When the rubber band feels tight, put the whole thing on a level surface and release.

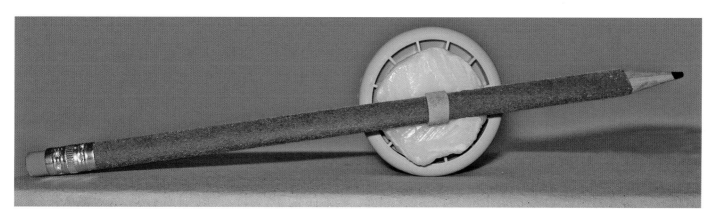

6 How far will it go?

What's going on?

We call the energy used to twist the rubber band in step 4 *potential energy*. When we release the tank, the rubber tries to return to its usual length and, as it straightens, some of its potential energy is converted to movement (*kinetic energy*).

What else can you do?

Your tank will tackle rough ground better if it has notches around its edge. Get an adult to help with a craft knife.

Jargon Buster
Torque is the special name given to a force that makes something go around.

Measuring Forces

To do scientific experiments, we need to measure things, often to make comparisons. Scientists measure force in newtons, but we can use our own units – marbles and centimeters!

The plan

We're going to make a measuring device and then use it to conduct a simple friction experiment.

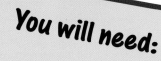

You will need:

- empty margarine tub
- 2 same-size elastic bands
- string, lots of marbles
- ruler, some shoes
- scales for weighing
- notebook and pen

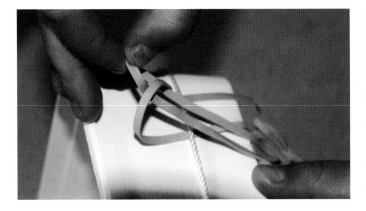

1 Thread the string through one of the elastic bands and tie it around the margarine tub. Attach the other elastic band to the first one to make a chain.

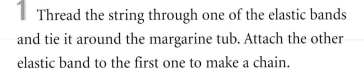

2 Put the tub on a flat surface. Lay the elastic bands out straight but don't stretch them. Put the ruler next to the bands so that the 0 is in line with the end.

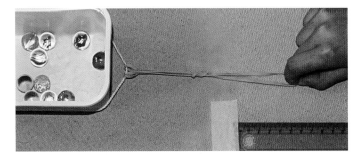

3 Put 10 marbles in the tub. Gently pull on the end of the chain of elastic bands, moving it up the ruler until the box starts to move. Make a note of where on the ruler the chain had reached when this happened.

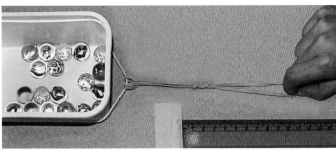
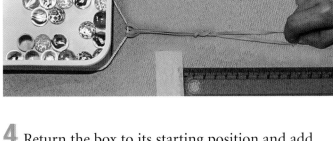

4 Return the box to its starting position and add another 10 marbles to the box. Pull on the chain and make a note of how far along the ruler it reaches when the box moves.

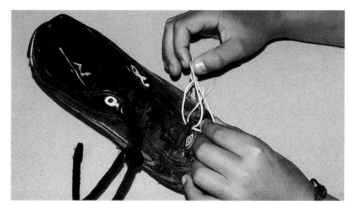

5 Which shoes do you think grip the best? Use the scales to find the heaviest shoe. Add marbles to the others to make them all weigh the same.

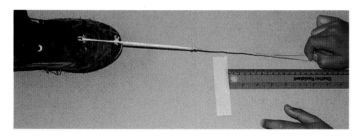

7 Pull on the elastic band chain and make a note of how far the elastic band has stretched at the moment the shoe starts to move. Repeat with the other shoes.

6 Take the elastic band chain from step 1 and attach it to the first shoe with a piece of string.

8 Place the shoes in order. How do your results compare to your predictions in step 5?

What's going on?

In the first part of the experiment, we see the effect of weight on the friction between the tub and the surface it rests on. In the second part, the surfaces that are in contact vary, while the pressure applied to them remains the same. The shoes that require the most stretch to move them have the best grip.

What else can you do?

See what you can do to decrease or increase friction. Put all your results in a table like this one.

shoe	stretch
Mom's sneaker	
Jane's sneaker	
my clog	
my soccer cleat	
Jane's clog	

Jargon Buster
Friction is the force that resists movement between two touching surfaces.

Air Force

How do planes stay in the sky? What invisible forces are at work to help them fly?

You will need:

- foam sheet (from a model shop), plasticine – about the size of a penny, pin, thread
- black marker, scissors, glue stick
- colored paper, pencil, tracing paper
- an adult with craft knife, paints, brush

The plan

We are going to show how well a simple toy glider can fly through the air.

What to do:

1 Use these drawings as *templates*. Copy the three shapes onto a sheet of foam.

2 Carefully cut around the shapes with scissors. Ask an adult to cut out the two slots with a craft knife.

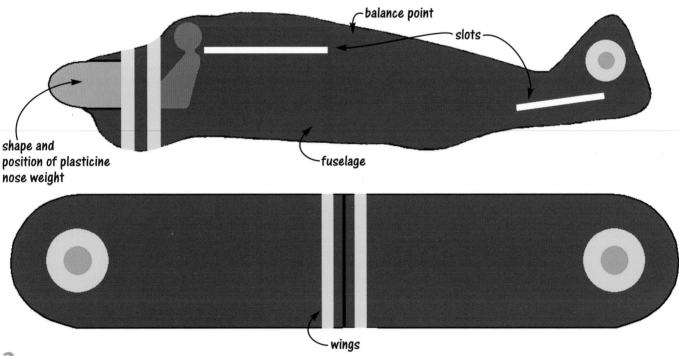

balance point

slots

shape and position of plasticine nose weight

fuselage

wings

3 Paint the flat shapes first. Apply markings after paint is dry using colored paper shapes and a glue stick.

tailplane

Add details, such as body panels and a canopy with a black marker.

Hang the plane from the balance point with a pin and some thread.

24

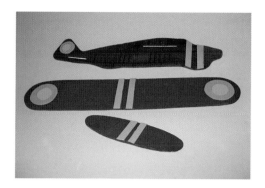

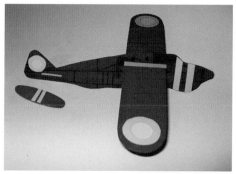

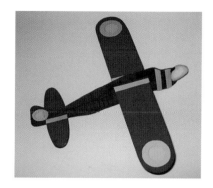

4 When all paint and glue is dry, push the wings and tail into the slots. Add the plasticine to the nose.

5 Move the position of the nose weight until the plane hangs correctly from the balance point. Send the plane off with the nose slightly down. Good flying!

What else can you do?

Help your friends make planes and have a competition for the longest (timed in seconds), highest and furthest flights!

What's going on?

The plane needs forward motion to thrust it through the air. The wings passing through air convert this force to lift, opposing the force of gravity. The tailplane and tail fin stabilize the plane, keeping it at the right angle to stay up. If the plane loses forward movement through the air, it *stalls* and drops.

Surface Tension

35 minutes

Look at a glass of water from the side. Look closely at the surface of the water. You will see that it is not flat but curves up at the edges. This is caused by surface tension, a force acting between the water molecules and the glass.

Experiment 1

The plan

We are going to show the power of surface tension!

You will need:

- thin cardboard, scissors
- soap, dishwashing liquid
- water in a bowl and a glass
- paper clip
- tissue paper

template

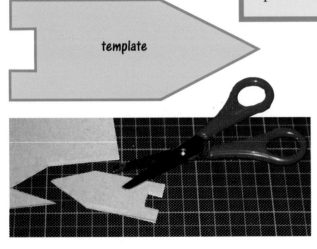

1 Copy this shape onto cardboard and cut it out.

2 Put the boat on the water and see what happens.

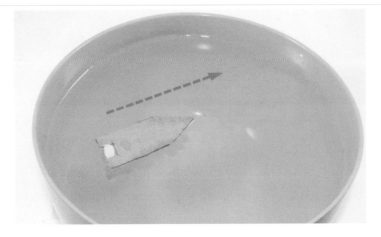

3 Take the boat out of the water and put a small piece of soap in the notch. Place the boat back in the water.

What's going on?

The first time we put the boat in the water, it didn't move because surface tension pulls equally in all directions. When we add the soap, surface tension at the back of the boat is reduced, allowing the boat to be drawn forward.

26

Experiment 2

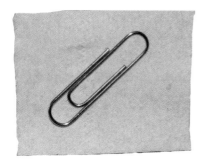

1 Take a paper clip and put it on a scrap of tissue paper.

2 Gently lower the tissue and paper clip onto the surface of some water in a glass.

3 When the tissue becomes *waterlogged*, it will sink to the bottom, leaving the paper clip floating on the surface!

4 See how quickly the paper clip sinks when we add a drop of dishwashing liquid!

What's going on?

At step 3, the paper clip isn't really floating. Surface tension is strong enough to hold it above the surface of the water against the force of gravity trying to push it down. The dishwashing liquid rapidly spreads across the water, destroying the surface tension, and the paper clip is no longer supported.

Jargon Buster
The surface of water in a clean glass is drawn up at the sides in a curve. It's caused by the tension between the water and the much denser glass. The curve is called a **meniscus**.

More Balloon Fun

15 minutes

We've used balloons in a lot in our experiments but there are still more things they can show us. Here are two forces at work.

You will need:

- balloons, one large balloon
- permanent marker, string
- an assistant, wool sweater
- kitchen scales

The plan

We look at the difference between mass and weight, then see the force produced by a static charge.

Experiment 1

1 Here's a big, empty balloon. It weighs just .7 ounce (.02 kg).

scales are not exact for weighing very tiny amounts

2 Now we've blown it up, and it seems to weigh about the same.

3 Your assistant takes the balloon and hits you in the back of the head with it!

What's going on?

The balloon doesn't seem to weigh any more after we've blown it up than it did before. It feels heavier than the empty balloon would when it hits us because it carries the mass of the air inside it as well as the rubber of the balloon, all propelled by the smaller boy.

Jargon Buster

Weight is how a mass is affected by gravity.

Experiment 2

1 Blow up two balloons and tie their necks. Attach strings.

2 With the strings at the top, draw a face on each balloon. Use a permanent marker so it doesn't smudge.

3 Find somewhere to hang them up, a doorway is ideal. Let them hang about 2 inches (50 mm) apart and see where they settle.

What's going on?

4 Rub the faces of the balloons with the wool sweater.

5 Let them hang free again and see how they behave.

In step 3, the balloons settle with the faces pointing in any direction. In step 5, the faces turn away from each other.

Rubbing a balloon with wool fabric produces an electrostatic charge on it. A similar charge on both balloons means that they will repel each other. The force should be strongest where the rubbing occurred, and so the faces turn away from each other.

Jargon Buster

Electrostatic charge is caused when an electrical charge is apparently trapped in an insulating material, such as the rubber of the balloon.

Flying Machine

Let's use what we've learned so far to help us build a flying machine. The big problem for heavier-than-air craft is gravity. Here's a way to use fresh air to beat it!

The plan

We're going to make a very simple hovercraft.

You will need:

- pop-top from a drink bottle
- balloon, small binder clip
- old CD or DVD (make sure it's not wanted!)
- rubber cement
- very flat surface, such as a kitchen counter or glass-topped table

1 Unscrew the pop-top from the bottle and make sure it's dry. Glue it to the CD or DVD, exactly in the center. Check that the top is closed.

2 Blow up the balloon and put a binder clip on the neck so you don't lose any air. Then fit the neck of the balloon over the pop-top and remove the clip.

What's going on?

The air escaping from the balloon can't easily get out from under the disc, so it forms an area of *pressurized* air. The disc is lifted and floats on the cushion of air.

3 Place your hovercraft on a flat surface. Open the top of the pop-top.

Glossary

accelerate (ik-SEH-luh-rayt) To increase velocity.

density (DEN-seh-tee) The compactness of something.

Hero's engine (HEER-ohz EN-jin) Invented by Hero of Alexandria, circa AD 62, a device that propels itself by shooting steam from one or more openings.

inertia (ih-NER-shuh) The way matter continues in its existing state, unless changed by an external force.

inflates (in-FLAYTS) Fills with air or gas.

interaction (in-ter-AK-shun) An action or effect between things.

kinetic energy (kuh-NEH-tik EH-nur-jee) Energy that a body possesses while moving.

lift (LIFT) Upward pressure on an aircraft wing caused by forward motion.

molecules (MAH-lih-kyoolz) Groups of atoms bonded together making the smallest units of a compound.

momentum (moh-MEN-tum) The quantity of motion of a moving body, equal to its mass times its velocity.

newtons (NOO-tunz) The standard international unit of force. It is named after the scientist Sir Isaac Newton.

observations (ahb-ser-VAY-shunz) Statements about what you have learned by using your senses, e.g., heard or seen.

pascals (pas-KALZ) A measure of force applied to an area. It is named after the mathematician Blaise Pascal.

potential energy (puh-TEN-shul EH-nur-jee) Energy in an object, such as heat in hot water or tension in a stretched balloon.

pressurized (PREH-shuh-ryzd) Having a force that raises or keeps pressure in something.

propulsion (pruh-PUL-shun) The action of driving or pushing forward.

stalls (STOLZ) In flight, not having enough forward motion to provide sufficient flow of air over the wings and control surfaces.

submerged (sub-MERJD) Put below the surface of the water.

sustained (suh-STAYND) Something kept going over time.

templates (TEM-pluts) Shapes that can be copied.

velocity (veh-LO-suh-tee) The speed of something in a certain direction.

volume (VOL-yum) The space occupied by a something or the space within a container.

waterlogged (WAW-ter-lawgd) Totally full of water.

Index

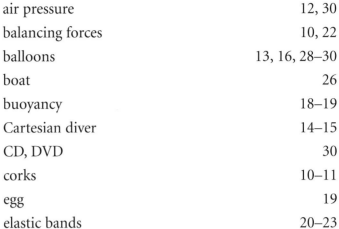

Web Sites

Due to the changing nature of Internet links, PowerKids Press has developed an online list of Web sites related to the subject of this book. This site is updated regularly. Please use this link to access the list:

www.powerkidslinks.com/scilab/force/